Coal Dust on Roses

Also by Susie Utting and published by Ginninderra Press
flame in the fire

Susie Utting

Coal Dust on Roses
last days of a mining town

Acknowledgements

I wish to thank my principal supervisor Gary Crew, and assistant supervisor Ross Watkins, for their encouragement and advice in the creating of the poems contained in this collection. They form part of a thesis submitted for a Doctor of Creative Arts at the University of the Sunshine Coast. A transcript of the full thesis is available on the USC Research Bank at http://research.usc.edu.au/vital/access/manager/Repository?exact=sm_type:%22Thesis+%28DCA%29%22

I am grateful for the financial assistance provided by USC for the publication of *Coal Dust on Roses*.

Coal Dust on Roses: last days of a mining town
ISBN 978 1 76041 022 3
Copyright © Susie Utting 2015
Cover photo: view (taken by the author in 2012) of Yallourn Power Station across the former site of Yallourn township

First published 2015 by
GINNINDERRA PRESS
PO Box 3461 Port Adelaide SA 5015
www.ginninderrapress.com.au

Contents

Prologue: Why coal dust falls on roses	9
Fading…	13
Full Bloom…	31
Withering…	59
Epilogue: Lookout	86
Notes	88

'When from a long-distant past nothing subsists, after the people are dead, after the things are broken and scattered, still, alone, more fragile, but with more vitality, more unsubstantial, more persistent, more faithful, the smell and taste of things remain poised a long time, like souls, ready to remind us, waiting and hoping for their moment, amid the ruins of all the rest; and bear unfaltering, in the tiny and almost impalpable drop of their essence, the vast structure of recollection.'
– Marcel Proust, *Remembrance of Things Past*

This book is inspired by and dedicated to the life and times of the people of Yallourn, and their town in the Great Gippsland Swamp, Victoria.

Foreword

Yallourn was built on the coal rich surface of the Great Gippsland Swamp in the Latrobe Valley of Victoria. It was envisaged by its founder Sir John Monash as a model town for coalminers and their families, a place where residents worked for and lived in houses owned by the State Electricity Commission. Situated sixty miles to the east of Melbourne, the interplay between town and country featured prominently. Carved from the bush, it represented a rural version of a garden city in Australia, its public and private spaces proudly maintained. From the 1920s to the late 1970s, inhabitants enjoyed this lifestyle until the SEC decided to dismantle the town to mine the coal beneath.

This book is not meant to be an accurate account of the town of Yallourn. As 'squatters' living there in 1978, my family witnessed its last days. We also witnessed the traumatic impact the demise of their town had upon the remaining residents. The poems in this collection contain my special memories of that time. A range of events from around 1975 to 1981 have been compressed into one year, 1978. Place names have been altered in order to avoid misrepresenting any person, time or particular event. Primary and secondary sources were extensively researched to provide factual details subsequently woven into a loose narrative of lyric poems, haiku and haibun – a Japanese literary form that integrates poetry (haiku) and prose in the same text. The evolution of haibun in English was researched for the exegetical component of a doctorate completed in 2015. Several examples of haibun are included in the last section of the book.

For anyone interested in reading more about Yallourn, the following were used in research mentioned above:

Fletcher, M. 2002, *Digging People Up for Coal: A History of Yallourn*, Melbourne University Press, Melbourne

Harvey, C. 1993, *Yallourn Power Station: A History 1919 to 1989*, State Electricity Commission of Victoria, Melbourne, Victoria

McGoldrick, P. 1984, *'Yallourn Was...': A Historical and Pictorial record of the functions, life and people of this 'deceased' town*, Gippsland Printers, Morwell, Victoria.

Read, P. 1996, *Returning to Nothing: The Meaning of Lost Places*, Cambridge University Press, New York.

The Old Brown Coal Mine Museum at Yallourn North contains a treasure trove of Yallourn memorabilia. Its library and helpful volunteer staff have extensive reserves of expert knowledge as most are ex-Yallourn residents.

The YOGA (Yallourn Old Girls Association) website provides amazing resources and a medium through which all who love Yallourn to reconnect and share memories of their beloved town.

Notes at the end of the book provide additional information for those who meet the Yallourn story for the first time in this book.

Prologue:
Why coal dust falls on roses

Gyres of incision and lateral intrusion from the highlands
sediments to the coast and further sweeps

giant eddies in floodplains, lakes, peaty swamps and marshes
boggy-spored
wombs from the

Eocene to the Miocene geological and climate gestating
thick brown pulmonaries

in the Valley and off the coast of Bass Strait
in situ 100,000 million

tonnes in seams that pancake from Traralgon to Yallourn
streams of carbon
as thick as

100 metres vertical and deeper 400 individual continuous
low ash coal flows all
borne on ceaseless tides over

eons of high seas rapid growth induced in swamp fauna and
flora
continuously flooding

pine and banksias that flourish to die then sink into the mud so
slowly smothering

leaves, bark, woody trunks and roots in a never ending
process squeezing
swampy fluids into a mighty river

that seeps through the marshes to spill lakes with more
strata heavy with dead trees and vegetating

undertows in the earth that shift mightily
enfolding hills to realign valleys that glide to cradle

The Great Swamp.

Dramatis arboreum

In the beginning –
black butt   mountain monarch
amphitheatre of hills   beneath

channels of tree fern   cooling
greenhood and maidenhair –
primordial arcadia

For a brief interval –
imported pleasure gardens spring
flushed with ordered finery

theatres of ash & poplar
vaulting sets of golden elm
& oaks   so

gently husked
by homesick thumbs
In the end –

brown empty stage.

'Coal dust blackened the washing as it hung on the line, and gave a grimy coating to flowers in the garden.'

Meredith Fletcher, *Digging Up People for Coal*

Fading...

branch outside stirring in the stillness of the empty room

                    in the petal fall
                              change of season
                steals the chill

autumn ash
      column of falling copper
drift in a single shroud

                              from the back veranda
                    a mating call
                                  the telephone

Report from a Besieged Town

(after Zbigniew Herbert)

I will try to be precise
but I don't know
when the end begins –

already the future here
where houses   whole gardens are dug up   no wooden tombstones
mourn when nothing remains

Dredgers clank –
clank through their teeth singing
mouths full of coal

In this season of intermittent brown –
outs   black outs   strikes almost every day
promises are broken like front fences   chimneys   whole kitchen walls
Our voices are never heard
by bureaucrats in sheepskin suits butchering at midnight
in cabinet yards

Our children run
over bare slabs   chipped
shadows of a nightmare

beyond the levelled corpse
Meanwhile the beast licks itself
clean   of remorse

Overhead a crow
crosses the landfall
where our future empties

into waiting trucks
I will write quietly   so my voice is loud
chirping in the dust

Above the town
cooling crematorium towers
this dark satanic mine.

Town Square

No cross roads connect
hotel & rail station
bus stop & fire brigade

Instead, a long straight line
spools to red brick public buildings –
churches schools library RSL

post office health centre &
in the middle
bandstand with Memorial Garden

…in wars fallen
Those who died in their beds
prop up tombstones

in the Haunted Hills –
buried among indifferent messmates
they brood like worms

some nights turning
towards the centre to learn
how they will remain

when the living leave –
dug up for coal.

The Library

This morning mist
stains roses brown?

Claret ash bleeds along the avenue
A thick brick building
walled with windows

thrusts demurely onto the square
Through its foyer we pass
a shoosh of readers in a silent glade

Veneer panels gleam
Marveer polish lingers
in mushroom mould of fraying spines

Queen of Dewey system hive
the librarian glares
from her high curved desk

Wooden floors echo with footsteps
in another chamber
I hear a silverfish sneeze

A class from the primary school
on a mat mute
listen to *Shy the Platypus*

We choose three picture books
The librarian archly states
Only people in the town may borrow here

We doddle home through the gardens
Laughter spills over
lawns of children & fallen leaves.

Back fill (i)

brown lignite bog is the youngest
softest crumbly coal of compost
                              trees   mosses   sages   sedges

all genus of quagmire
creep into bedroom cupboards
                              seep through tongues
of my best suede shoes

briquettes break apart
                        coals prodding
awake dead plants

where a river is diverted
                  beneath the ground
into a sinkhole dissolves

orchids love bogs   *beauty & the beast.*

Kinder

The room is large
flooded in natural light –
wide window eyes in pastel

slits of blue and pink
From a ring of children
the teacher smiles with her eyes

Everyone on the mat
The wooden floors are electrically heated
Past the doll corner

toy town kitchen stove & sink
elfin easels stand to attention
in newspapers spread on lino floors

Monday morning smocks
primary colour clumps
hang in a well behaved row

frozen on steel hooks near the door
On the playground
lawn reclines a huge cotton reel

ancient conveyor belt
spool from the power station
At the back gate

a chain of silky oaks
swing soft
tintinnabula.

Back fill (ii)

snug hobbit homes –

these attic houses   steep

                                       pitched

                bright orange roofs

with sturdy weatherboard sides   hardwood floors

    children   hide   seek   window eyes   a secret moon

they grow on stout red gum stumps

                up

where bannisters slide

                        to

attic bedrooms

        but

will a briquette heater

      melt

this winter pall?

Post Office

> Postmaster
> franking stamp for a
> skull
> Handle with care

We wander down to the PO...
twin brick replica of the bank
on the other corner

Terra cotta tiles at the entrance
Inside jarrah floors that echo
like the library

Silverfish here too in the piles
Return to Sender & Address Unknown
in a special bin

A white sign declares *The Postmaster General requests cooperation in attempts to forward mail to former residents If anyone knows their present whereabouts please...*

No home deliveries here
now the population shrank
so letterboxes disappear like rose bushes –

this week hydrangeas
dug up for their brilliant blue
from the copper below

Private Letter boxes line up
stiff little soldiers in a tidy
troop on the left side wall

The main counter is a superb swoop
of hoop pine with a writing slope
too high for children

The Postmaster slides
the parcel over to the edge
Your grandparents spoil you…don't leave it out in the rain!

In the park on Centreway
we rip off the brown paper wrapping
Inside a red wooden engine

                      perhaps…
                            over lunchtime tea
                      he reads the town…

Early Morning Perambulation

disturbed root
    in summer blooms
leafless stem

I've been told by our neighbour that our garden *used to be*!
the best in town – *Mrs R. consistently collected prizes* but I
notice gaps in the hedge *rhododendron azalea japonica daphne*
missing along the side brick paths
I ask & she says *garden thieves!* roaming empty blocks on
moonless nights raid our floral treasures so *Mrs R. took her
favourites with her*
She left behind the back fence *Albertine* climbing rose so
savage too cruel its thorns no wonder she didn't bother & on
the driveway *Black Beauty* too big
Perhaps she may remember this last redeeming flush of ebony
buds before winter

waft of lemon
    scented eucalypt
        balm for tears

                autumn chill
                    in the warmth
                        of my breath

Back fill (iii)

gripes…   empty briquette bag on the back veranda
hot water heater with no split wood
a city *Everhot never runs out*

days when the fog never lifts

pressure cooker pea soup explosion
scraping bacon bones down kitchen walls

men who never shut doors
when it takes all day to heat this house –
men who never notice draughts?

the crow that steals eggs from the chook shed
a twin-tub washer eating socks.

Poetic Pruning

never try   to move   a poppy

    Wise gardeners know they rarely bloom in neat beds
    with straight smooth sheets & enjambed edges so
    instead I rip irregular roots from half dashes in back
    door phrasings and slash from every tiny Grecian ode
    its shining seeds before discarding on my compost
    pile – while all over unplanted caesures sweet sap
    unfolding sing purple snatches of narcotic vowels in
    blooming whorls to poke through
    my untilled page

    opium plot   *an ordered scheme*   *chaos seeds*

swirling leaves

                            slowly fall

                                    into empty pages

                  unable to read thoughts I write only words

Cumquat Brandy Liqueur

My house is fecund
sunny nooks of bay –
silled windows where I cradle
unset moons

Cumquat-scented verse
I pluck
in autumn garden golden chill
I prick
rusty darning needle
through
their unformed cowls

I plop
silken velvet globes
squished adjectives and nouns enjambed
in cool glass jars

Perfume bombs away they swell
ticking round   still   sugared
in utero my brandy
poems float…

I should have made jam.

                            slipping over into it winter's spoor

Mushrooming

                      death caps born under oak kill in hours

They grow best
where a river winds with willows that seep & creep
into banks

across the paddock I see
magic circle of Saffron Milk Caps
under pines
on the wind break side
rings & rings of Slippery Jacks
& Giant Fields

                      white nipples in green velvet probing

In patches of dry manure
withered crones with ink slit eyes
battered hats
poke through among fontanelle of morning babies
I gently stroke
under pucker/pink chins before
I pop   with a tug
into the bucket

I hear
warm butter froth in the pan
the moment folds
silky black
        sleep awake I would have heard white cat prowling

as fog creeps in
mute   no sun   winter
milkers' gloom   wrapped
in a wet sheet
shroud   I wander
along the barbed wire
scramble through   as
afternoon
         slipping
deeper
       in.

Hospital

the fog endless
                     silvery   bewilder   ness
only my eyes
          are working

James coughs
all day
like a seal
like most at Kinder

*not to worry it's normal as soon as the nights grow cold here
Friar's Balsam in boiling water towel over his head & let him
breathe the steam or leave him in a hot bath till the whole room
mists up…sometimes this helps*

so we try both ways but
it doesn't
still
chest heaving   rasping like a little door
swinging

                     fog tonight

                     in our bathroom   crazy

                     clouds of thought

The nurse gently burbles
don't mind the mask
she'll fix the strap so
his throat will fill
soft warm fog   *early this year* her ward
half full tonight with a new pod

                        flock   fold   bob

whole rookery of pups & whelps
swimming in blameless seas

soon
James breathes deep
no more heaving

        the terror

fully inhaled

                    folds its wings
One day we dig up daffodils…

…James, Lucy, Jack and me
in fine warm rain
Each bulb a baby buried in the bush
they clutch each other
vertically in naked sleep

until

temporary tombstones of past pioneers
they poke grey fingers through forgotten lawns
in dim-cool hobyah gullies
in a foreign land.

Full Bloom...

        sleep in the fleece of delusion

    dusk falling in the hedge row creeps

dark matter is dark   energy   in a black hole   slowly

        buried

                resurrecting

'1951–1952: Yallourn dwellings 1062. Population: Town 4967. The SEC gave notice in August 1961that Yallourn township would have to be removed for the coal underneath it.'

Colin Harvey, *Yallourn Power Station: A History 1919 to 1989*

'Are local places important? How can assessors or friends gauge the significance of a place to people who may scarcely realise its value to them until that place is threatened?'

Peter Read, *Returning to Nothing: the meaning of lost places*

Playing Fields

A landscape mirror
once upon a time reflected
eight perfect ovals   each
a homesick dream

perfect county pitch with white picket fence –
enchanted pleasure garden

Here, in raucous dying light   still
strong enough to scratch out
soft blue eyes
they listen for adored refrain –
faint chock of leather on imported willow

Hear too – click of croquet stick
rolling bowl on jack
catgut on rubber
all   drifting up through end of day

playing still
in shift overalls before the walk
slowly home   through
Broadway gardens.

Snap Shot: a) 1930's Young Woman with Cow, Milk Bucket & Dog

Why are you here?
the Jersey in the middle
asks through dark liquid eyes

To the left
a milkmaid waits in sackcloth
dress stiff above her calves

See where her hand
fondles a velvet neck
in intimate caress

Feel how every
morning those fingers stroke engorged
drooling teat how

the other hand clutches the bucket handle
as if
she fears to waste a drop

Zoom to the background
forlorn farmhouse with no front garden
only doomed paddocks

Cut to the lower corner –
the dog is only a head & paws
but you can hear him thinking

about last evening
how close that front hoof –
dare he enter the picture?

Take in the dusty track
twisting to the right horizon
Imagine the girl

driving in a truck
milk cans chinking to the town where doorsteps of jugs &
bottles wait for her
stumble through the dark

Imagine the girl
walking to the railway station –
never riding home

Instead she lingers
in sepia forever wondering –
did I rinse out the butter churn?

b) 1950's The Paper Boy

On the seat you perch
feet on the front tyre rim
pudding basin short back & sides
Mum gives all her boys

Forward you lean
arms crossed like you're tough
but the shy half-smile
doesn't lie

You sit proud
on your Coronation model Malvern Star
no gears but a packing case tray
Dad made for the paper run

You wear a surplus army jacket –
between your knees
a brown leather pilot helmet   fur flap turned back
like you're ready to fly

Through the frost you're off
load of *Sun* or *Argus* sometimes *Age*
each morning 100 houses street names & numbers
pencilled over the headlines

Russians Race to be First in Space   *Labour Party Split Widens*
You steer with one hand
roll up the paper with the other then jam
between gate & fencepost

Some mornings
papers soaked by the time you reach Driffield Road you know
Mrs Green will be on her phone
You coast on

along Outlook Road
latch hook rug of orange rooves   green ovals
distant patch of snow
but you peddle on

down to the crackle of briquette heater
dry clothes & Mum waiting
Porridge with Currants
worth all of 12/6d a week

Here you belong
snapped between black & white
in a world never turning grey.

c) 1950's Student Nurses with New Record Player

The nurse far right on the floor
stares directly at the camera
eye daring

her parents in a different state
to disapprove   *loose lips sink ships* her father always boomed
evil will come from the jitter bug   all those wanton
American hips

but she doesn't give a hoot
since her sister died
in a backyard 'butcher shop'

The nurse on her knees on the left-hand side
seems to be praying
this photo never reaches Charters Towers

They boast there
she's completing her honours degree at Sydney University –
when she writes home
she doesn't mention
in theatre last night with her mask in place
the new intern smiled at her   couldn't see
her face   how plain

The nurse at the back
is already taking charge –
notice how exactly she positions the stylus
in the right groove –
future *Matron with excellent organisational skills*

Now look closely to her left –
the smiling pretty one with her
jaunty cap & no top button
Scatterbrain   Dizzy Lizzy   how she will weep
next week
when she doesn't bleed

In the top right corner
who is the plumpish nurse?
like someone underwater   out of breath   about to burst
off the rails   laughing
all the way to Brisbane/London/penning witty scripts to
bloom in
comic skits/ Ab Dab as Finch & Sanders/grab
the limelight
at last
have the last laugh.

d) 1979's Butcher Shop

The woman with the pram
loathes stench of raw meat but
her husband loves his steak
well hung

The old woman in the dark coat
searches for two plump shanks
for her dead husband's dinner

The window is a farm of green
plastic shelter belts for paddocks of lamb
chops/ mutton forequarters & cow
eye fillets/inkstain kidneys/cerise T-bones

All lie beneath
a downpour of sausages
fat English/skinny Polish/liverwurst brown

Inside the shop the sawdust slips
clumsy boys up   hurling them into the counter
where the butcher rolls his marbled eyes –
smugly taps his boxer's nose

His apron is an atlas of blood
islands in a dark sea
how wild this morning

the steer's kick –
so heavy the veal heart
sluiced insanely through
his meaty hands

Behind the counter stands
the block   Amadeus lake of smooth dry wood
where backbones are cleaved

The scales of life are tilted here –
pigs hang out along the back wall
glassy-eyed   cavern-mouthed   but their feet
are missing

arranged in a neat front window field
ankles tied with string
When you leave the shop

take your change warily
as the apprentice grins –
rub your silver coins along the parcel paper
wipe away the blood

Walk home before your liver leaks.

e) 1970's Swimming Pool Swimming Pool Clock

Ten o'clock
The turnstile groans –
pressure cooker pleasure of young limbs thrusting
out to the sun

Fervent young bodies push each other –
how long underwater
breaststroke to the deep end before
bursting up
to fling a spray of liquid diamonds –
how far from the top board
plunge through a cloudless sky before
silencing jeering crowd

Twelve o'clock
In the minnow pool
(hidden by the tree midground) –
hear the chirp of toddlers
in hoops of water   mouths exploding   laughter bubbles tangled
in shallows tumble
until they cling
limpets in toweling shells
on mothers' knees

Three o'clock
The lifeguard struts –
tanned ripple stretching torso before
horn on zinc cream lips he drawls
No dive bombs at the shallow end…you know the rules…that boy in striped shorts…report to the office…now!

Six o'clock
The siren screams
All lovers under boundary trees   scoop up
your towels   undo your knot-tie
limbs & wend to the exit gate
linger   eyes & kissing mouths enlarged then
twist apart   wander
hungry   home

Eight o'clock
Along the down of lawns
soft slide of light now held in printer's ink –
see how the foreground
follows blackness of the passage of the sun how
triangular oblivion rubs out
bright day

Midnight   Swimming pool clock, your time is up.

f) 1970's School Musical Oliver

Front spot centre stage
Titch is about to say
Please, sir…

while upstage all the boys
breathless from 'Food Glorious Food'
drift twenty sets of eyes towards
first spot as the *mood colour* swings –

Titch & Ando gaze stage left where
Bumble Mr T pot-bellied science teacher & Widow Corney
librarian Mrs H serve the gruel

The front stalls know the plot
sick to death if the truth be told   Saturday rehearsals
disrupt team selections (mainly for the Thirds) but on cue
they will all gasp

at Oliver's audacity
Hard to believe
Mummy's Boy   top of the milk Titch

will grow so fast in Form Four
his knees will ache
all year long he will wake
most nights screaming

but he will jump so high –
touch Commonwealth Bronze
Medal in 1982

Meanwhile upstage right
the kid behind the keg
watches the hand pass a note
to the Form Five with his back to the audience

'Bullseye threw up in the wings…'
so the cast exit left
when front lights *fade to black*.

(Sikes' terrier Bullseye/Digger is proudly owned by the Artful Dodger/Tom Bridges from 2C.)

g) 1970's Back Row Boys

Roll call from Left-hand Side

Nathan Nerd
bright spark in Pure Maths/Calculus but
his glasses are in his blazer pocket so
he cannot see the flash

Farm Kid Barry
up at five today for milking
will 'wag' tomorrow –
sale yards day with Dad   sweet scent of trampled hay
fresh turd under his boots –
will leave soon to work with the stock & station agent –
buy a farm on the Murray

Angelo the Wog
new kid from the Tech
shocked them all last week –
bowled Mr Boyle for a duck in the teacher/student match
thrashed the bullies in a fight behind the shelter shed
but no one even he dreams he will play
full forward
for Collingwood

Class Clown Kevin
half-smirks –
Hydrogen Sulphide beacon he left in the science room
drawer will ensure the whole school on the oval till lunchtime –
reek of rotten eggs so glorious
like the night
he stuffed up the chimney in the boiler room –
his candlewick bedspread
charred beyond all recognition

Gavin the 'Girl'
tries to smile but it's hard
squashed between two apes –
they tore Dusty Springfield from his locker door & trashed
Dr Who into a breezeway drain
He dreams how he will write his Edinburgh comedy hit
Kevin & Brian *Downunder Dumb & Dumber* but
he doesn't dream
Brian is killed
on a motorbike in 1978

Peter the Jock/footie hero
is seriously considering his Saturday strategies –
lead for the ball or feint back
to the goals?
ask Debbie Divine (end RHS second row) to the school
dance
or Rhonda?
but he doesn't run fast enough to stop
the unexpected pass –
father of a baby girl
spittin' image of Debbie   everyone will say

Terry Titch
star of 'Oliver'   town hall encore record holder
cross country champion 2 years in a row
never suspects he will grow
6 feet 3 inches tall   even his mother…

Jason tries hard
working for the gang –
dunks new kids' heads in the toilets & smokes
Drum rollyourowns behind the tractor shed
but he tries too hard
dobbing Kevin for the egg gas so
no one really cares when he goes next year

Teacher's Pet Philip –
who here will ever read
his poetry collections
published by Melbourne University Press & so admired
in the ivory tower where he eventually resides
except English teacher Mrs C –
dies in 2012 of breast cancer
never knowing how much he loved her
musty shelves of Auden & Ashbery

Did you notice
only one row of boys?
The others have left for the Tech or briquette factory –
so the three lines of girls must dig up
husbands in the open cut or leave
the picture forever.

h) 1970's Family (i)

She stands
half in and half out of the frame
backlit by the kitchen globe

She laughs
straight in to the lens because she's happy

her four sons sit
together today as if close-knit –

bearded engineers in Aran jumpers
all her work   their double cabled cardigans

How untroubled their eyes appear
through John Lennon glasses – how clear

the future if they don't look
into the flash

Their wives are hard helmeted
matrons with bobbed hair and self-satisfied expressions as if
their crochet pattern babies are somehow
special here –
a family christening perhaps or a first birthday snap so quick
buzzing past like flies in summer rooms

Her husband is leaning
into the hollow of foreground blur

smiling perhaps because he doesn't know
he is not safe –

he must hold his breath like he's underwater or he will lose it
suddenly in ten years – on the golf course of all places…

She stands
tartan scarf knotted at her throat   still

as this tableau
lingering in the shutter.

1970's Family (ii)

You stand in a warm blue
jumper I knitted that
four year old boy –

best friend beside you
on the high back row
You seem to tilt –

no rail to stop your fall
The sun is hidden
in the peppercorn tree

You search for me
with my dead father's eyes
brown – a thread of green

In the background
an open space you reach to meet
mother of your son

At your throat
the last row in the pattern   there
I dropped a stitch.

From the kitchen sink…

The garden is a filmy scarf of pinks and blues
around a pea-green pond

The flitting drifts descend
round tea time –

blue wrens and silver eyes
dart in clumps of Sage
I watch them bathe

      – the greatest privilege.

Broadway

Its three main stems
bleed to every part of the town

Streets flow easy grades and gentle curves
for billy carts and freewheel bikes to crash
through westerlies

The main artery brims
scarlet geraniums on nature strips, standard
Coronation roses

weeping cherry between
Queen palm & silky oak
There, bog deep in asphalt circulates

a star-crossed heart.

Back fill (iv)

In 1934

water...
fills
       the bowl called the Great Swamp
decants
       continuous rivers
blocks
       leaves/debris in conduits so
power station condensers stall

water...
washaways
     into the open cut
scours
    top soil into sludge
masses
mud   all over

pools
    at the bottom
metres below deep oceans

water…
casts adrift
                five people on a kitchen table
maroons
a ninety-two-year-old woman in her brass bed
strands
   horses in haysheds   sheep on tussock islands
floats
   floats
     a boat rowed to a farmhouse

water…
dumps
    a town high & dry   nary a drop to drink
    nothing to burn   no briquettes

in a sea of darkness.

Submerged Rerun

When where we went leaks through illuminates & memory spins in
along the track & dips sweet into the valley bleached
foothills autumnal tunnel slowly revealing gum-licked messmate horizon as
it sweeps beneath the gravel so suddenly
lurch-sharp and we drive how slowly must it slice
how deep through the crystal do i breath-hold
in fright my water babies in the back seat the world
drowns in luminescence pristine clear as
bohemian glass but no time to slip slide down now firm behind
steering wheel push buttons but no doors no windows open locked
Davy Jones dead no way out the wet & now so cold i
primeval urge clawing i pull push back space window out until
we bob lightly on water.

Topography

On your map
you may see the head of a ram –
Murray River border
leister northern back of woolly hills
down to a straight merino nose

tipping east to the blue
round the muzzle
coastal inlets   promontories   indentations
tracing out two decent chunks
of bay before the scraggy underbelly
in another state

On a map
you see his luxuriant jowls –
high micron count wool
best grown here or
on the breastplate over the Western heart or
cheek dimples over
Ninety Mile beach

In the Great Swamp
fibrous carbon density winter is bitter cold and spring rains
heavy
with lamb

On my map
I see the feet of mothers
foot rot swollen bags sadly swinging
udders through flooded creeks and in summer
stench of fly struck drought

Those who travel far
up rivers where the squench of mud & rolling crests of dark
green surge to banks motionless under the moon
silence sliding away in thin layers of sanity

wade ashore with me –
glimpse beyond broken jaw of landscape   jagged dream
shuddering on a midnight stroke
my map.

Withering…

                        wind chimes
                echo of voices
                                  in another room

last leaving the door heavier to shut

to learn
                what you really don't
                              want to know

from the future
                a storm drifts in
                                    hope?
                          pours down

pushing an open door why is it so hard…

            the past a window
                    traced with sliding fingers
            in pulverised sand

Memorial Garden

Red granite woman
kneels forever –

her wreath too late
to mourn the living

garden town   now dead
in a brown coal grave

In sculptured beds
eternal red roses

bloom   on
marbled stems.

Back fill (v)

any night…
…from the shed roof
 brush tail possums
                            leap to feast
                on the weeping cherry

…a male koala coughs
                    heavily
outside the bedroom window

…on the compost heap
                New Holland mice
scurry through kitchen scraps

…in his grass lined burrow beneath the rose garden a native rat
nibbles on a pumpkin lump

…pre dawn high in the lily pilly magpies
tiff

…near the chimney under a rafter the ship rat
outsider
            inside
suckles her thirteen babies.

Rats

Rattus Rattus (introduced black rat)
Rattus fuscipes (native bush rat)

That morning
inside the potting shed –
mayhem of ceramic shards
shredded paper bags
seed pods with neat Halloween
holes in her butter pumpkins
Empty bag of blood & bone –
plastic skin discarded in the far corner
where piles of olive pip
droppings defile her watering can

Is this the answer
to her garden Somme?
dugouts   underground secret tunnels
looping to the back fence
No wonder her raspberry canes are dying
roots gnawed clean
by these trench raiders
hidden in her own backyard

That afternoon
she brings home poison
quicker than strychnine
the label stresses so
mindful of her children she hides
a small powder hill
beneath the 'spider tree' where webs
impervious to her white oil wrap leaves every night
in neat grey parcels

Next morning
she finds the small chunk of fur –
brown short tail flat against the earth
translucent ears like stranded beach
shells upturned   baby-pink feet
The tiny slanted nose barely twitches
Eyes flooded with blood
twist towards her
The final shock is quick –
her victim calm at her feet

That night she reads
she contaminated the order
in swampland   spoiled its rhythm
vast & ancient
Invaders never dig deep
only briefly inhabiting
the surface of realities

Later that night
through a window she sees the moon
cross the mud sky like a silver tail –
less jellyfish   starfish creeping   along   beside
before they sink
into gravity

She sees how a tide of people might rise
then ebb
all their scratchings dissolved
in the pristine beauty
of the swamp

At dawn she beholds –
skimming over pebbles the glimpse
of a rat
out from under.

Saving the Wisteria

Dad digs
Tough as old boots 'Wisteria floribunda' won't hurt another move…
He digs two feet

out from the trunk wrist-thick
Loves the winter here…
Branches twine clockwise

anticlockwise over the garden shed
Shame to do this now…in full bloom
Bu not much choice…soon

this backyard…dug up too…
He dips the wounds
where the shovel sliced

in Yates rooting powder –
tucks her in a cracked jardinière
When you move…she'll cover any old shed by spring

I grab the secateurs & cut
long pendulous racemes –
purple fragrant cascades

I cradle them into the kitchen –
arrange them in tall cut crystal
vases for the dining table

I bring Dad tea & scones
in a mist of mauve perfume.

Golden Years

Mean fat boys'
big sticks
stir the ant nest...

       Iris and Ted live in Maiden Street
       Their garden today a sensual delight to wander through
       early roses gardenia late daphne too in a northern
       corner
       Last month Iris slipped on the mossy bottom step &
       broke her arm
       Years ago Ted was injured in a dredger accident &
       wrecked
       his back which made him a pain in the neck he loves to
       tell everyone
       Ted needs Iris
       He has no idea how to boil an egg so neighbours drop
       in with meals/chop kindling for the chippie heater
       Ted and Iris have never saved a penny
       They spend anything left over from his invalid pension
       (after paying the rent & shopping) on trips interstate to
       see grandkids & Iris's sister who married a sandgroper
       & still lives in Kalgoorlie
       They have never saved & never had a mortgage
       Should have bought that block Iris says but no need
       back then when everything was provided here
       When they eventually leave they will receive a small
       sum for relocation of residents who lived here before
       1969 but it's not enough for a deposit on one of the
       Golden Years units past Haunted Hills
       Iris's friend Molly says everybody loves it here at

Golden Years but she still misses her old house
Ted says They can take me out of here in a box
Iris sighs & nods

…little creatures go around
in circles   wandering   wondering
what happened to their home

The Death of the Wanderers

Once upon a garden
they fell in love
in a fugue of asters thistles goldenrod
red clover & temperate verges of milkweed
for their babies

who grew on leaves
of lilac smooth as the tawny lace orange
veined with black
their mothers wore

Once upon a night
the milkweed soured as the children heard
birds cluster in the trees flowering
in the gathered chill

On this metamorphosis too
young they missed the flight – the shift
pattern of instinct set
by another circadian clock

Now in silken pods they twist
here with claws too blunt   to   scratch   out
gaps   chew through   to
memories they never reach

Instead they wander
into another consciousness only
lit by sudden flashes of over summering
beside a beach

For these wanderers there is no migration.

The Fox

Down old ways he swings
brush sweet with freshly crushed grasses
into the underbelly

where the passionfruit climbs
over an orchard fence
Umbrella moon

pokes through the stick finger
branches of fruit trees
bitten like a nervous girl's nails

back to the quick of spring
He glides towards the cherry blossom
bride near the chook pen fence

where he begins to dig
Alone in the dark
sweet tang of broken hay & blood

he feasts on the tiny flapper
boa of bantam's wing
The tin-topped shed is screeching

so frantically a light blinks on
the house veranda
He bunkers low in rosemary

till the moon shifts
his moment to reclaim
the coal black town.

Playground

What's the time, Mr Wolf?

Time to swing
in spring through
almond blossom storms
high on sturdy boughs where babies sleep
in prams beneath

Poke through
secret place in the privot hedge
into a sunbeam room
where mothers chat in perfumed drifts
jonquils sweet peas grape hyacinths
no *Atropa belladonna* here

Time to skip
summer yonnies & brinnies across
fat goldfish dozing in green
water lily fans

Build a fort in the sand
pit with a well drained moat
beneath the spreading English elm
in luscious shade

Time to fling
autumn leaves to the cool day moon

In winter see –
saw with a new best friend
in a whirl of gumnut
plots & bunyip stories

Throw your tor
on the 8 in the hopscotch square
twist round & jump
before

the lambs are murdered.

Garden Stall

kidney seeds asleep in a twin womb

>Inside the Hall
>stalls of potted plants/seedlings in trays/cuttings bare
>rooted stand along walls & between makeshift aisles
>where gardeners gather to exchange/give away/select to
>carry home each other's treasures
>Vegie Seeds...
>tables groan with rows of jars pumpkin Butternut/
>Golden Nugget/Queensland Blue & beans all sizes
>Lazy Housewife/Seven Year Runner/Rattlesnake &
>more
>Seeds in thumb-stained earth-smeared envelopes
>plucked from recesses dark in potting sheds & paper
>brown bags carefully labelled Purple Congo/Pontiac/
>Goldrush lettuce Bloody Butcher & wide array of corn
>Bulbs etc in another corner...
>wicker baskets of rhizomes tubers freesia iris bluebells
>tulips lilium
>Soon string bags rattle with pods/old soup cans brim
>with slips of Apricot Queen/Double Lilac/White Fairy
>Rose & ivy geranium climbers...

>from broken homes for strange new walls

corm caskets   prematurely borne   open wounds

Saving the Roses

disillusion   disillusion   so hard to pull   out   of

> We all arrive with gloves spades secateurs
> We wait by the Floribunda beds opposite the bus station where
> rows of Iceberg standards white & pink alternately also wait
> to be rescued…
> Grandiflora roses stand too especially Queen Elizabeth
> & there is keen interest to get to work to save all these beauties
> Bourbon roses are long time favourites…Empress Josephine's gorgeous Souvenir de Malmaison
> & Cardinal de Richelieu…the way he turns so magnificently from mauvish pink to mauve then deep purple
> Dedicated members of the Horticultural Society
> set to work destroying gardens they have adored for generations
> The annual show used to be so popular…
> Biggest Pumpkin or Best Decorated Cake to adorn a mantelpiece
> …no more a Junior Princess of Flowers with bunch of Black Velvet from her back fence
> Kevin Heinz was the chief judge once…
> We all watch *Sow What*
> Arthur is a dahlia maniac
> Wife Joy breeds African violets & her progeny sit proudly on town kitchen windows
> We dig up bushes & wrap them in hessian sheets

Children with little spades dig
know how to shake gently soil from the roots
Those with rakes tidy up
Afterwards…
down to the hall where
CWA ladies serve tea & scones with apricot jam

perfumed keepsakes dug out by the roots

Back fill (vi)

fire...
burns homes with briquette heaters
                                                                                     exploding
ceilings with coal dust   black ink inches deep

fire...
jumps the highway on Black Friday
                                            scorching
longer than a week   so wide   fierce
                                                                           licking
briquettes in trucks near the factory

fire...
sweeps through timber country
                                                          consuming
hedges   wooden sheds   old outhouses

fire...
leaps the river to the open cut
                                             smouldering
underground
            over centuries.

Smoke and Mirrors

2 o'clock
night after night I expect her
return with her grey tail lingering
in doors with her tongue
rubbing raw
old sores in a tic
behind my eyes

I listen
for paw pad in the hall
stray scrape of extended claws
in corners in my brain
I listen hard
for the plasterboard to crack
fear from fact like a poker
shot hot through the head

She preys on
soot fall of doubt –
scent of smoke-filled dread
flaking ash on crazed reflections
Hestia without her hearth…

4 o'clock
mice scratch in the wall
the blackboard window yawns at the moon
lanterns on the lemon tree

In another room my dead mother
cries in her sleep
my husband beside me yells and kicks
a winning score
our children smile in uncharred dreams

6 o'clock
garden stars of jasmine open
as the moon slips
down leaving chalk
streaks of dawn

My dressing gown hangs
on a crooked hook behind the door

I pad in slippers to the kitchen –
the stove is cold.

Christmas Party

we trip into the future hesitant at crossways

> The Fire Brigade puts on the best party
> Lamb on a spit & butcher Bert's best sausages
> 5 o'clock
> The fire station siren blasts & wildly excited kids take off down the streets
> The fire truck bell rings along the Avenue
> Already the park is overflowing with families sprawled across lawns or under elms

golden conversations in salad days

> 6 o'clock
> The six huge doors of the fire station open
> The fire siren blares
> Santa on his way yells someone with large lungs
> Everyone in a circle   little ones in front A final roar as the truck pulls in
> Santa has a multi-capillaried red nose & a belly that shakes
> 'like a bowlful of jelly'!
> Has everyone been good this year?
> Yes! the kids scream
> 7 o'clock
> The lamb is carved
> Soon the band starts up &
> Barry from Open Cut Maintenance belts out the crowd favourites
> 9 o'clock
> We trail home through the silent night

Hotel Funeral

(auction of the goods & chattels of Yallourn Hotel)

The remains are laid
out in carpet soft saloons
where velvet lounges

line the mirrored walls
They repose with silver browed teapots
on silent counters

Dining chairs
barley sugar legs upturned
rest on satin oak

tables all through
passages with shroud tablecloths bearing
caskets of cutlery

We reverently admire
before final decisions as
the gavel falls –

each stroke another little murder
on the auction table
Later down Broadway

family cars & trailers nudge into funeral file
as women shuffle
home to half packed rooms.

Back fill (vii)

Arriving...

1948

He could see   through
windows   back
yards of homes   peculiar clothes
lines   sheep on low brown hills
dead trees

strange grey leaves

A loud laugh split his first
kookaburra dawn

No fences
so cows
during the night   but he liked   that

Winter
      here
no snow
           now

only rain
grey   slow   seeping
rain

He likes that...

Departing

1978
>The remains of twilight
>dredge
>into the valley
>
>>I walk back
>>down the hill to a rubble site…
>>piles of broken bricks/beams/verandah posts/naked
>>drainpipes
>>The entry steps lead nowhere
>>Our chook shed lurches precariously towards the back
>>fence
>>chicken wire sagging like tired elastic in Granny's drawers
>>One jagged corner remains of the lounge room
>>interior yellow painted bricks chipped & stained where
>>we hung our Madonna with Goldfinch print bought
>>eons ago in the Uffizi
>>The front dining room wall stands stiffly
>>soot-smeared Arc de Triomphe to the fallen   our town
>>windows now glassless eyes gaze blindly into motionless
>>streets
>>A pile of chipped orange tiles still clutters the driveway
>>but
>>Hestia our wood combustion stove heart of home is gone
>>Across abandoned sites
>>I notice the cooling towers & power station
>>stacks brutally carrying on curling clouds into an
>>indifferent sky
>>Along the nature strip
>>crows moan in the plane trees
>>I will not brood on the uselessness of all this…

cobwebs   spin

                                away

            cross our hearts

'By 1978, the population of the town was less than a 1,000. It was no longer a pleasant place to be living in.'

> David Longmore, *Planning Power: the uses and abuses of power in the planning of the Latrobe Valley*

Mire

River fog
muffles the mud sky
trailing out the mystery

We wait here
between shadows
following shifts as clouds drop

through gravity to their source –
among the vapours
but in it lost so

we prey the wrong way
Gently the river moves
over eons the rump easing its ooze

further into the centre
Together with the worms we star gaze
blindly not knowing

which way
to squirm on the surface
waiting with the ancient

twisted roots slaters grubs microscopic lice carbon corpses
for the mud
deep whisper/answer.

in deserted rooms
      no clocks
strike the hours

Buying the Farm

On a spur of the moment we buy the old farmhouse with its magic carpet views
On this mild spring day the world lies at our feet in a patchwork of paddocks quilting the Valley between Mount Baw Baw & Strezlecki ranges
The kids go crazy
darting with swallows through the tottering hayshed
We wander down overgrown paths in the tangled garden sasanqua camellias double spiraea & crab apple trees
Twisting around blackberry canes half-choked rhododendron pom pom & lilac through the orchard we track in knee high grass to find ancient plum cherry cumquat quince pear apple & stunted lemon trees
The old farmhouse has two open fires & a slow combustion stove
The previous owners stripped the hallway walls back to the hessian while the bedrooms are an unfinished mix of hessian & newspaper
The children are deciding where to put their beds & toys in the glassed-in veranda round the west side of the house
In the front room D. reads out to me a headline from 1935 Italian invasion of Abyssinia
Our youngest is playing with dead daddy long legs near the back door
I pick him up then find an old straw broom & sweep them down the steps

                                          pansies have taken to their beds

Epilogue: Lookout

There is a road   still
over the hill

to cooling towers and tainted cloud
in a coal dust sky

A sudden wind
whips so hard on the edge
you won't stay

long

Information Board tatty
maps faded places and dates
missing whole periods…

To the east you will glimpse
feather duster chimneys of Hazelwood power
aloof Loy Yang

Below the lip of the hill
pick up   out   two trails of liquid

amber in the avenue
you dwelled on
a lifetime

before

those threads fade
into the cyclone
lychgate to a dead town

Climb down
through

the graveyard of messmate —
you don't stay

long.

Notes

Pages 10. The Great Swamp: Gippsland in eastern Victoria has always been wet. The Great Swamp was riddled with bogs and unseasonal floods. The first settlers followed the Old Sale Road north of the present Princes' Highway to find a relatively dry route to the east. Over the twentieth century, the Main Drain has provided permanent drainage.

Page 16. The cemetery for residents who requested to be buried near where they had lived is on a hill approximately five kilometres away, adjacent to the small community of Hernes' Oak in the Haunted Hills. Although marked on early town plans, a cemetery never eventuated in Yallourn itself.

Page 20. Yallourn attic houses can still be found all over Victoria. Built in the 1920s and 1930s from a design by the architect A.R. La Gerche, they provided homes for SEC workers and their families. Originally their weatherboards were oiled dark brown but later most were painted. Upgrades to plumbing and wet area furniture were carried out after World War II when the town was sewered. During the dismantling of Yallourn after 1969, attic houses could be bought for $4,000.

Page 21. The Post Office design was the inspiration of Sir John Monash, who requested that its architecture complement that of the State Savings Bank on the opposite corner in the town square. It was thought only appropriate that the building be constructed of local bricks and roofing tiles. The interior included a substantial blackwood staircase and comfortable first floor living quarters for Postmaster General staff.

Page 23. Gardens (residential) in Yallourn were highly maintained and valued, both within and outside Yallourn. In the last years of the town, garden theft was a common practice, carried out by those unentitled to unusual species and rare plantings. Yallourn varieties of old-fashioned roses, both from public and residential spaces, mysteriously appeared in home gardens and for sale in nurseries throughout Gippsland. Taking pride in one's residential garden was part of the concept of the ideal garden town.

Page 29. Hemophilus pertussis (whooping cough): in the early 1900s infant mortality due to pertussis was considered so serious that it was classified as a notifiable disease in all Australian states and territories from the 1930s. In 1954 it was included in the routine immunisation schedule for Australian children. However, in Gippsland, especially in the Latrobe Valley winters, cases routinely filled local hospital wards including Yallourn.

Page 33. Public Spaces in Yallourn were integral to the concept outlined by Sir John Monash in 1920 of building 'an ideal garden town', giving workers the opportunity to live their lives in a pleasant home environment close to their place of employment. It was also anticipated that such an idyllic circumstance would obviate workplace unrest; for example, mining strikes. The Australian model would be far removed from the harsh actualities of life in English coal mining towns.

Page 42. The Yallourn pool remained open until 1980. It was one of the final closures in the town. The swimming pool clock stopped forever at 6.41 on that day.

Page 54. Major floods were a regular threat to Yallourn. The open cut was drowned in 1934 and its giant dredgers silenced under three feet of water. Recent floods include 2012 and 2013.

Page 61. Rattus fuscipes, the native bush rat, is primarily a burrower, strictly nocturnal and generally a herbivore. The tail length is shorter than the head and body length, which is a useful diagnostic feature. Rattus Rattus is the introduced ship rat or roof rat and is a long-tailed generalist omnivore. They are serious pests as they eat birds and insects and invade human spaces.

Page 68. Monarch butterfly (Danaus plexippus) is a milkweed butterfly (subfamily Danainae) in the family Nymphalidae. It is perhaps the best known of all North American butterflies. Since the nineteenth century, it has been found in Australia and known here as the Wanderer. It regularly migrates through Gippsland to breed on Raymond Island near Lakes Entrance.

Page 75. Fire was considered a serious threat in Yallourn. The fire station was manned at all times to avoid outbreaks in the open cut. The town was threatened during bush fires in 1939 and 1944. House fires were relatively common.

Page 79. Yallourn Hotel was situated on one of the town's main corners opposite the railway station. It opened in 1928, with its first Christmas dinner such a success that it became a tradition. The original building was added to in 1937, 1945, 1956, 1959 and 1966 in response to the growing numbers of patrons over the years. When the hotel closed, everything was auctioned. Pieces of hotel memorabilia take pride of place in many ex-residents' homes. The hotel building was demolished in the early 1980s.

Page 80. Displaced persons on the first boats to arrive in 1948 were 'Balts'. Some were sent to work in the Yallourn open cut for a weekly net wage of four pounds fifteen shillings. 'Welcome to Little Europe' was the sign on the gate of their camp outside Yallourn. Italians, Maltese and some Finns were there already but soon outnumbered by later arrivals, including the British.

www.ingramcontent.com/pod-product-compliance
Lightning Source LLC
Chambersburg PA
CBHW062140100526
44589CB00014B/1638